SLASH

An Intimate Portrait

Photography by
ROBERT KNIGHT

Foreword by
RONNIE WOOD

Preface by
JOE PERRY

Text by
RICHARD BIENSTOCK

INSIGHT
EDITIONS

San Rafael, California

INSIGHT
EDITIONS

PO Box 3088
San Rafael, CA 94912
www.insighteditions.com

INSIGHTEDITIONS.COM

FOR WEB EXCLUSIVE CONTENT!

ROOTS of PEACE ⊕ REPLANTED PAPER

Insight Editions, in association with Roots of Peace, will plant two trees for each tree used in the manufacturing of this book. Roots of Peace is an internationally renowned humanitarian organization dedicated to eradicating land mines worldwide and converting war-torn lands into productive farms and wildlife habitats. Together, we will plant two million fruit and nut trees in Afghanistan and provide farmers there with the skills and support necessary for sustainable land use.

Manufactured in China by Insight Editions

10 9 8 7 6 5 4 3 2 1

Slash's cat, Fidel Kitty, takes a stroll past the most iconic hat in rock and roll.

Contents

FOREWORD BY RONNIE WOOD 13

PREFACE BY JOE PERRY 15

INTRODUCTION BY ROBERT KNIGHT 17

The Early Shoots

20

Slash's Snakepit and Velvet Revolver

32

Out and About

44

Fairfax High School

76

Portraiture

84

Recent History

112

ACKNOWLEDGMENTS 143

COLOPHON 144

Foreword

SLASH HAS A MAGICAL ABILITY to adapt when he plays guitar. He slides seamlessly into any situation, be it musically or in terms of personality, and is compelling in both ways.

His massive talent on the guitar comes from his being an inquisitive child, always looking to learn and striving to achieve his own style of playing. I know 'cos he used to cop my licks while peeping over a chair when he was little . . . now I cop his licks!!

He has been a friend of mine for many years, and fortunately we still manage to keep weaving our guitars together, wherever we may be on the planet!

—Ronnie Wood

Preface

I FIRST HEARD SLASH IN 1987. Aerosmith had been back together for three years, and we were starting to find our groove again. We were finishing a new CD and planning a tour. Geffen, our label at the time, was buzzing about this new band, Guns N' Roses. Having seen so many come and go, including us, I was ready for anything. I got their album and played it top to bottom and, needless to say, I was blown away. I knew this one was here to stay. These were great tunes, with a great singer, sound, and swagger, but with a slight prejudice for guitar that I could hear running through the whole record. Slash's guitar playing, supported by Izzy, held my attention from beginning to end. He seemed to have captured all the sound, energy, grit, and attitude of the greats before him, while managing to make an indelible statement of his own. A cornerstone that any player worth his salt would make a pact at the crossroads for—and this was only his first record! But Slash is the real deal. From his name alone, to his trademark hat, shades, sneakers, and low-slung Les Paul, he is the iconic guitar man.

Alongside—or, I should say, in front of—him, capturing his career on film, is the man with the camera, Robert Knight, whom I consider to be one of the top rock photographers of all time. So much of what Robert does, aside from his obvious technical skill, is about being in the right place at the right time. Rock and roll is all about spontaneous energy. Robert's talent is to feel the ebb and flow of this energy and to know when to hit the shutter. He has proved this time and again. As Slash carved his spot in the pantheon of iconic rock personalities, Robert was there to capture it. And as their relationship has grown, a magic has happened that you can get a glimpse of in these photos.

This book is a great window into a world that exists sometimes in public, but mostly in private. I could say this is a typical collection of photos capturing a typical rock star's life, but there is nothing typical about Slash. He is his own man, at one with his guitar and set on following his rock-and-roll muse, with his close friend Robert right there to immortalize it. These are magic moments. This collection will hit you like it did me, right in my rock-and-roll heart. It's the real thing and it made me smile.

—Joe Perry

Introduction

IN MY LIFE synchronicity is an important thing. Nothing is random.

When I was young, my parents were missionaries to Hawaii. My dad was Southern Baptist and worked as a minister at a Japanese church. I wasn't allowed to listen to rock music, and movies were off-limits. TV was highly restricted. But I had a small crystal radio, and I remember hearing a song by John Lee Hooker. It scared me because I thought, My parents are right; this *is* evil. It felt creepy. It felt like I was into something dangerous.

I didn't want to be in Hawaii. I hated heat. I didn't surf, I didn't like water, I never went to the beach. Can you imagine living in Hawaii and never going in the water? It was a miserable place for me.

But not all the time: One afternoon in 1965, I was walking through Waikiki and came across some discarded magazines in an alleyway. They were British, with pictures of some very weird-looking people in some very weird-looking clothes. I picked them up and began reading about these rock bands. There were the Pretty Things, the Yardbirds, the Who, the Kinks, the Stones. And the photos blew me away. We had Peter, Paul & Mary and *Hootenanny* and all this other bullshit. We had the Beatles trying to hold your hand. But the Rolling Stones didn't want to hold your hand; they wanted to hold your *sister*.

One of these magazines had an ad for a record store in England where you could buy new-release records through the mail, and so I began building a secret collection. I convinced the teachers at my high school to let me play this music over the loudspeaker during lunchtime. I became very hip—I was a DJ before we even knew what a DJ was. But after a while all the artists at my school realized I didn't play guitar, I didn't write poetry, I didn't paint. I had no real reason for being in the room other than I had a really cool record collection. So I was pushed out of this little circle.

My ticket out of Hawaii and into a new life came when I was sixteen and working as a travel agent near my home. After a year on the job I acquired agent's discount passes and used them to fly to London. I don't remember quite how it happened, but I found myself staying with a family in Putney. One day they said to me, "We look after a photographer's studio, and they're making a movie today. Would you like to go down?" That movie turned out to be Michelangelo Antonioni's *Blow-Up*, about a photographer in London shooting rock bands and models. And wouldn't you know it? The Yardbirds were in it, too. A bell went off in my head and I said, "There's my passport to being in the room. I want to be a photographer."

Jeff Beck

In the summer of 1968 the Vietnam War was raging, and my parents wanted me to go off to some kind of college so I wouldn't get killed. I noticed that Bill Graham was booking all these great new acts into the Fillmore West, so I convinced my parents I had to enroll at the San Francisco Art Institute. Then I went down to the Fillmore and shot Jeff Beck on his first tour in America with Rod Stewart. Jeff was twenty-four at the time, with no shirt on and wearing suspenders. I was nineteen, with some Tri-X film and a Nikon F camera. David Hemmings had used a Nikon in *Blow-Up,* so I figured that was the gear you had to have.

My next subject wasn't too bad either: Jimi Hendrix at the Winterland Ballroom. I just walked in with my camera and went right up to the stage. No one stopped me. This was in the days before people went to shows with cameras, so security must have thought, He's with a newspaper or from somewhere important. I had only one roll of Tri-X with me. I didn't know— thirty-six pictures seemed like a lot! I took fourteen and my jaw hit the floor.

Through some connections I had come into contact with Jann Wenner, and in early 1969 I begged him to send me to the Whisky a Go Go to shoot Led Zeppelin for *Rolling Stone.* It was their first show in Los Angeles. I wasn't old enough to actually get into the venue, so the girl at the box office called the Chateau Marmont, where the band was staying, and got Jimmy Page on the phone. Jimmy said, "Send the kid over here." I spent the day with the band and they brought me down to the gig. Then I traveled with them to San Francisco and shot them again at the Fillmore.

I called a promoter friend back in Hawaii and told him he had to book this band. He did, and a few months later I left school, went home, and picked up Led Zeppelin at the airport in Honolulu in my Volkswagen. They walked off the plane carrying the master tapes to *Led Zeppelin II* in their arms. We hung out in a rented house at the foot of Diamond Head for a few days. I landed them an interview with the island's only FM station. I took them surfing.

It was around this time that I decided I was going to be a rock-and-roll photographer. I would take around my portfolio and people would ask, "Well, who've you worked with?" And I'd say, "Um, Jimi Hendrix, Led Zeppelin, Jeff Beck . . . " "Oh, okay, fine. You can shoot." It was that easy.

But I never worked *for* anybody. At the same time I was shooting bands, I was also making great money as an advertising photographer. In Hawaii, an ad agency once called and said, "If we gave you one thousand dollars, would you shoot a loaf of bread for us?" I thought, That's crazy! But from there I took on jobs for all these other companies. My commercial work was the only way I could underwrite my ridiculous appetite for following around rock bands. Because I had the hookups, I could go to Seattle on an ad job and then hang out at the Edgewater hotel with Led Zeppelin or fly to London with Delta and shoot Jeff Beck.

This was the way I did it for years—the Rolling Stones, Aerosmith, Elton John, the Faces. None of this stuff appeared in print. I took the last shots ever of Stevie Ray Vaughan, minutes before he climbed aboard that helicopter. I had met him through Jeff, and he was a friend. It broke my heart when he died. I wouldn't let those photos out for years.

Jimi Hendrix

Almost nothing of mine was made public anyway. Maybe one shot of Jeff ran in *Rolling Stone*. They never ran the Zeppelin stuff. I would get the shots and then put them away. I never did it for the money or the fame or the controversy. For me, part of being a photographer was knowing when not to shoot, when to put the camera down and when to protect the artists' privacy. I didn't care about it as a career.

But in the mid-eighties I finally reared my head. A friend of mine needed an amplifier, so I walked into the Hollywood Guitar Center on Sunset and said, "I have a bunch of really cool photos. Can I trade you for an amp and a guitar?" They looked at my portfolio and said "Sure." Then they asked if I wanted to shoot their first RockWalk, which was happening that same day. I said, "What's RockWalk?" That afternoon I snapped photos of Eddie Van Halen and Les Paul jamming their hands into wet cement. I've photographed every RockWalk since, and I'm now the codirector of the event. A few years later, Guitar Center also began exhibiting my artist photos in their store windows and on exterior walls. Today, I have more than three thousand massive images on display at locations around the country.

My work with Guitar Center is what led me to Slash. In 1990 a Guitar Center representative called and said Guild was looking for a photographer to shoot Slash for an ad campaign. Would I be interested? I showed up at A&M Studios, where Guns N' Roses was in the midst of recording the *Use Your Illusion* albums. I expected Slash to be this scary guy, but he was a *kid*. He came out to my car, grabbed all my gear, and carried it inside for me. That shocked me.

Jimmy Page

There's always been a charisma, a presence, a true sense of self-realization about Slash. In all the years I've known him, I've never heard him complain; I've never heard him shout; I've never seen him have a rock-star moment. There's a calm within Slash, even as there's this insanity that revolves around him. He is truly the eye of the hurricane.

And everyone knows it. Here's a story I've never told Slash: A few years ago, I was with Jeff Beck in LA, where he was scheduled to play the Greek Theatre. Slash called and said, "Robert, tell Jeff I want to jam with him tonight. I want to play the encore." I didn't want to get in the middle of Jeff's business, but Slash kept on me. So finally I told Jeff that Slash had called. "Oh, cool!" he said. "How is he?" "Good," I responded, "and he wants to play with you tonight." And Jeff stopped. "Oh," he said. "There's nothing like playing ninety minutes and then having a guy with a top hat come out and steal the show!" Needless to say, Slash's charisma is not lost on Jeff Beck.

It's not lost on anybody, myself included. Over my lifetime as a rock photographer, I've amassed upwards of a quarter of a million images, a figure that's still growing by fifty thousand frames a year. I'm proud to say that a good number of those photos chronicle my relationship with Slash. He has opened his professional and sometimes personal world to my camera's eye, and in my own life, he has on more than one occasion been there for me in ways I never would have expected or could have imagined. As far back as that introductory shoot at A&M Studios he felt like a kindred spirit. More than twenty years on, I'm certain he is.

1

The Early Shoots

IN THE EIGHTIES I wasn't into the whole Sunset Strip rock thing. But just living in LA at that time you knew who Slash was. You would hear stories. The first time I became aware of him, I was in the Valley buying a bottle of wine at a liquor store, and the guy behind the counter said, "Slash was just here." I went, "Slash? What is *that*?"

During the early days of Guns N' Roses, the hair-band sound was happening in LA and I really rebelled against it. It just was not my thing and I didn't want to shoot it. I thought, Guns N' Roses, is that one of those bands? Then in 1989, I saw them open for the Rolling Stones at the Los Angeles Coliseum. It was just raw and chaotic and messy and great. I didn't know what was going on. I thought, This is the shit. This is the Stones. This is Led Zeppelin. This is as fucking rock and roll as you can get. And it's really, really *real*.

Before I finally met Slash at A&M Studios a year or so later, I only knew of him what I had seen and heard from a distance, which sometimes could be a little frightening. But I found him open and easy and incredibly professional. I had two immediate impressions: One was that I realized I had never seen his face before; he was like Cousin Itt from the *Addams Family*—I never knew what was under the hair. Also, while he's a gentle guy, he has a handshake like a vise. I thought he was going to crush my fingers!

During the session we talked about Jeff Beck and Jimi Hendrix, and Slash told me about his father, who he said was also a photographer. He put me at ease. We got some great shots—he even smiled in some of them, though he may have asked me not to use those. But there it was, Slash just beaming with his twelve-string Guild.

We did the shoot in less than an hour. I probably only needed a few minutes. Another thing that sticks in my mind is that the whole time we were working, there was a video playing in the background of a woman having a sex-change operation. It was just running in the studio, with no one really paying attention. Bizarre, but that was the Guns N' Roses world.

From there Slash and I became socially friendly. This was due in large part to my work with Guitar Center. Slash is perhaps the definitive representation of the modern-day iconic guitarist, and his image looked great in a store window or plastered on the side of a building. So there was always a pretext to do another shoot, and we developed a relationship.

A Guitar Center project is probably what brought me to the Palace in Hollywood for a 1995 session with Slash. He had a gig that night with Slash's Snakepit, and we spent the afternoon walking the halls. We found a foyer on an upstairs floor and decided to shoot in the windows. There was a great skyline in the background, which you don't usually see in LA. It was almost like looking out at New York City. I took out my camera and Slash sat down on a windowsill, Les Paul in hand and Gitanes cigarette hanging from his lip. A classic Slash pose.

Toward the end of the session at A&M, I had Slash pose for a few shots with his Les Paul for a project I was working on with the artist Jim Evans. Together, Jim and I produced a series of limited-edition hand-printed silkscreen lithographs with thirty-two layers of color, sort of an extreme take on the Andy Warhol thing. I shot Slash in both black-and-white and color, using whatever backdrop I could get in place quickly. Later on, Jim and I turned this particular image into a piece of artwork. There are a lot of little symbols hidden in the background; Jim likes to incorporate elements from a subject's life into his designs. If you look closely, you can pick out a snake, a motorcycle, a bottle of Jack Daniel's, and a few other things. It's a gorgeous piece. I have a thirty-by-forty-inch print of it hanging in my house. Slash signed it: "Dear Robert, those were the daze . . . "

2

Slash's Snakepit and Velvet Revolver

IN THE LATE NINETIES Slash focused much of his energy on his Slash's Snakepit project. Around the time of the band's second album, *Ain't Life Grand*, he called and said, "Dude, I don't have any budget, there's no record label, I'm financing this thing myself. Will you do some shots for me?" Of course.

He brought the band to my old photo studio, located at the Third Encore studio in Burbank. We took some group shots, and I also did a solo session with Slash. He was wearing a sort of see-through mesh shirt and a little black derby instead of his usual top hat. I've always been struck by his look here. It's not harsh. In fact, it's actually quite soft, almost model-like.

I remember this time as one of tremendous uncertainty in Slash's life. He was working with different musicians and going through changes with managers and labels and other business entities. It was a period of real upheaval.

A few years later, when he began playing with the guys who would become Velvet Revolver, it was obvious that things had changed for him. I had been living not far from the rehearsal studio in LA where Slash stored his gear, and I would stop by often because there was always something going on. He and the rest of the band were in a constant search for a lead singer and there was a steady stream of interesting people coming and going. He was excited.

Eventually Velvet Revolver hooked up with Scott Weiland and released *Contraband*. They experienced a lot of success. In October 2004 the band scheduled a surprise show in LA—a free outdoor gig meant as a thank-you to the fans. They had planned to stage it at a few different locations and finally settled on a parking lot at the corner of Selma and Ivar Avenues in Hollywood. Slash called me up and said, "Would you come? Bring your camera." They let me in early and I planted myself down front.

They played a forty-five-minute set for about three thousand kids. I've shot Slash many times with Velvet Revolver, but on that night, I could tell he was genuinely happy. The band had just gotten off the ground, the record was doing great, and they knew they had a good thing going. The show was amazing—at one point they even stopped traffic and began playing in the street. It was pretty wild. In general, there was a very powerful and explosive thing about Velvet Revolver. A real volatility. Maybe in the end it was a little too volatile.

There was such great onstage interaction between Scott and Slash that night. It was the classic singer/guitar player pairing, but in a much different form than Axl and Slash. Scott was a more sexual being and in a very androgynous way. He really did almost slither around the stage. I've always felt one of the issues for any singer with that big frontman ego is, What do you do during those long guitar solos? But Scott supported Slash and connected with what he was doing. It was a real moment where the circle felt complete again.

3
Out and About

SLASH IS A GUY WHO IS FOREVER IN THE MIX. Sometimes it's of his own
doing, but often it's just because people want him around. If you have an event
happening, and it's a rock-and-roll event, he's one of the people you look to.
And in LA, there's always something going on.

In 2007 Slash was inducted into the Hollywood RockWalk. I had
wanted it to happen for a long time, and, as codirectors, Guitar Center's Dave
Weiderman and I set it up. That year's group of inductees also included Ronnie
James Dio and Terry Bozzio. Slash came with his wife and sons. He was doing
Velvet Revolver at the time and Duff and Scott came down to support him.
Mike Clink, who produced *Appetite for Destruction* and the *Illusion* albums,
was also there. Lemmy Kilmister turned up, too.

Sometime later on, Slash and I were at the Hollywood Guitar Center
and I suggested photographing him next to his spot on the RockWalk. So
he crouched down and put his hand in his cement imprint as I shot away.
While we were doing this, a kid nearby was looking at the imprints of these
legendary guys, just dazed by it all. He didn't even realize that here was one
of the actual legends, kneeling right in front of him.

The kid probably didn't make the connection because Slash wasn't "in
character." When you really get Slash out and about, he doesn't have his top
hat on. He doesn't have his hair in his face. It's tied back and covered by a
backward baseball cap. That to me is the real Slash. That's the relaxed Slash.
But most people wouldn't recognize that guy.

I've had the opportunity to see that guy a lot, but I don't always *shoot* that
guy; it doesn't always seem right. Many years earlier, I spent a week at a house
in Hawaii with Jimi Hendrix. The same house, actually, that Led Zeppelin
had rented when they came to Honolulu to play that first show. For the entire
week Jimi was just relaxing. He generally laid by the pool in his bathing suit,
hanging. He wasn't in his gear, and he didn't have his guitar. I didn't take a
single picture of any of it. I don't think Jimi would have wanted me to.

Similarly, I think back to all those times I was around Slash and never
pulled out a camera. It wasn't always appropriate. It wasn't the be-all and end-
all of our relationship. It's something I feel about all the artists I'm closest to.
I'm a photographer, but I think it's important not to *always* be a photographer.

This was taken at the Revolver Golden Gods show in LA. Slash's wife, Perla, was excited that Jack Black and Kyle Gass from Tenacious D were there, and I saw her taking photos of them. So I said, "Why don't you jump in and let me get one of all of you?" Slash was behind them grinning about the whole thing.

The combination of Slash, Ronnie James Dio, and Terry Bozzio at the RockWalk was really surreal. We always try to get a lot of press at these events, so we tend to put together some interesting groupings. But the guys got along really well.

Slash and Lemmy are longtime friends. Lemmy lives up behind the Rainbow on Sunset, and they used to hang out together over there. I'm sure there are some wild stories to go along with those times.

Mike Clink produced the consummate Guns N' Roses sound on *Appetite for Destruction*. He and Slash have remained good friends through the years. Mike is one of the real good guys in rock and roll and Slash just loves him. I thought this was a real poignant shot.

STORYOFTHEYEA

DAVE WEIDERMAN

Everybody always claims to know Dave Weiderman because they think it'll help them get a discount at Guitar Center. They'll come in to the store and say, "I want the Dave Weiderman deal!" But not that many people actually know him. So one day when he wasn't there, Slash sat down behind his desk and put his feet up, and I took a picture. I put it up online and wrote something like, "For anyone that thinks they know Dave Weiderman, here's what he really looks like!" Slash laughed his ass off.

Guitar Center hosts a room backstage at the Grammys every year, and in 2005 I was there with Dave Weiderman when Bono walked in. He had organized a performance of the Beatles' "Across the Universe" to be staged that night to aid UNICEF's tsunami relief efforts, and he needed a place to rehearse. Dave told him he could have the room as long as I could take pictures. And Bono said, "Fine." So in came Bono. In came Steven Tyler, Stevie Wonder, Brian Wilson, Norah Jones, the guys from Green Day, Slash, Weiland, all these big names. I pulled everyone together for a shot, and it looked like an updated version of the *Sgt. Pepper's* album cover. I remember at one point Bono wanted to change some of the lyrics to fit the cause, and everybody said, "No, you can't do that! Those are John Lennon's words!" An amazing moment.

This was at the Golden Gods show. Alice Cooper performed with Slash that evening, and Johnny Depp showed up to play with Marilyn Manson. I was backstage when a security guy said to me, "Johnny Depp would like you to bring Slash to his dressing room to take a photo." So I told Slash and he said, "Tell him to come down to me." He laughed but eventually we made our way over to Manson's dressing room, where this was shot. Slash went in first and I followed a few minutes later, took the picture and split. Almost immediately everybody wanted the photo. I walked back to my hotel with Alice Cooper that night and he said, "You've got to get me a copy right away!" By the morning it was all over the world.

Teddy "Zig Zag" Andreadis used to be the keyboard player in Guns N' Roses. He was helping out as a counselor at the Rock 'n' Roll Fantasy Camp in Las Vegas, and he had a team of kids that he was teaching songs to. Slash came down to jam with them. They did "Paradise City" and a few others. A cool day.

Scott came down to the RockWalk with Duff, which I thought was a nice moment. This was at a time when there was still some camaraderie between Scott and the rest of the guys in Velvet Revolver. I thought it was pretty cool of him to show his support for Slash. And if you look closely, the photo of Slash on Scott's laminate is one of mine as well!

In 2001 I helped organize *Cars & Guitars of Rock & Roll*, an exhibit at the Petersen Automotive Museum in LA. Slash had a great collection at the time, and he brought down two of his beautiful vintage models: a sixties-era Lincoln and a late-thirties Ford. I took him up to the roof of the museum to do this shoot, and he posed in front of his cars with his Guild doubleneck and some other guitars. I remember being up there with a friend waiting for him to arrive, and he came around in one of these classic cars and drove right into a wall. We were like, "Woah!"

In 2009 Slash played a Slash & Friends show at the Mirage in Las Vegas to celebrate the hotel's twentieth anniversary. An incredible list of stars came out—Courtney Love, Rick Nielsen, Joe Perry—and the pool area was turned into a big concert venue. During soundcheck, Slash and Joe were onstage together, and at one point they were just talking. Funny enough, I think they were waiting for a singer to show up. There are many people—Beck, Hendrix, Page—who have had a major impact on Slash as a guitarist. But as a pure influence I think Joe Perry may stand taller than anybody. There's something about his style that really rubbed off on Slash. This shot captures a real moment where you can see the friendship and ease and respect that exists between them.

For many years Ray Charles was involved with the Blues Lab, which helped expose young kids to music and the arts. In 2003 Slash told me he was doing something with Ray for the program, so I went down to Ray's studio in LA to watch him and Slash play with these kids and teach them a few things. Ray was sick at the time. He'd come in for a bit, leave to go lay down and then come back. Slash jammed with him on a version of "Let the Good Times Roll." Duff and Matt showed up, too. It was a pretty extraordinary thing to watch. The kids all played it cool. They must have been thrilled, but they didn't show it.

4

Fairfax High School

IN 2008 AND 2009 I conducted interviews with some of my artist friends for *Rock Prophecies*, a documentary on my life as a photographer. I had Jeff Beck, Steve Vai, and Santana involved, and I knew I had to have Slash. For his scenes in the film we wanted to stage something compelling, and Slash suggested, "Why don't we break into Fairfax?"

Fairfax is a high school in West Hollywood that counts a lot of famous musicians among its alumni: Anthony Kiedis and Flea from the Red Hot Chili Peppers, Phil Spector, Warren Zevon, and, for a time at least, Slash—until he was kicked out. In a social studies class one day, a teacher singled him out and said something along the lines of, "Look at this guy. Longhair. Total slacker. Probably a musician. He'll never amount to anything." Apparently Slash picked up a desk, hurled it at the teacher, and left. That was the last time he stepped foot on the grounds.

Slash decided he should return. He said, "I haven't been there in more than twenty years. Maybe I'll drive my car down the hallways." Not too long after that, I found myself helping him sneak his custom Aston Martin Vanquish onto the Fairfax grounds, where he proceeded to take it for a spin through the outdoor halls. I rode shotgun. After a bit of this, he parked the car and we got out. Slash grabbed a guitar case and pointed to a small stage at the top of a set of stairs. He said, "This is the place where I played my first show. Right here." He sat down on a step, lit a cigarette, pulled an acoustic guitar from the case, and started playing. He probably sat there for twenty minutes. He was so perfectly still that the ash stayed on the cigarette. It just hung there.

By this time it was late and the sun was beginning to set. I was shooting at a ridiculous exposure, thinking, There's no way these pictures are going to come out. But Slash kept playing, so I kept shooting. Somehow the pictures turned out great.

Eventually, a few security men for the Los Angeles Unified School District came at us. They couldn't believe we had made it onto the grounds. I headed them off. They began asking for permits and all these things we clearly didn't have. So I said, "Look, I'm shooting a big rock star here." They asked who it was and I told them. That was enough for me to talk them into allowing us to finish up. In return, they asked if Slash would agree to do an event for the alumni association. "Sure," I said. As I was walking them around to where we had been shooting, I sent Slash a quick text: "We're coming back to you. Whatever these security guys ask you to do, just say yes!"

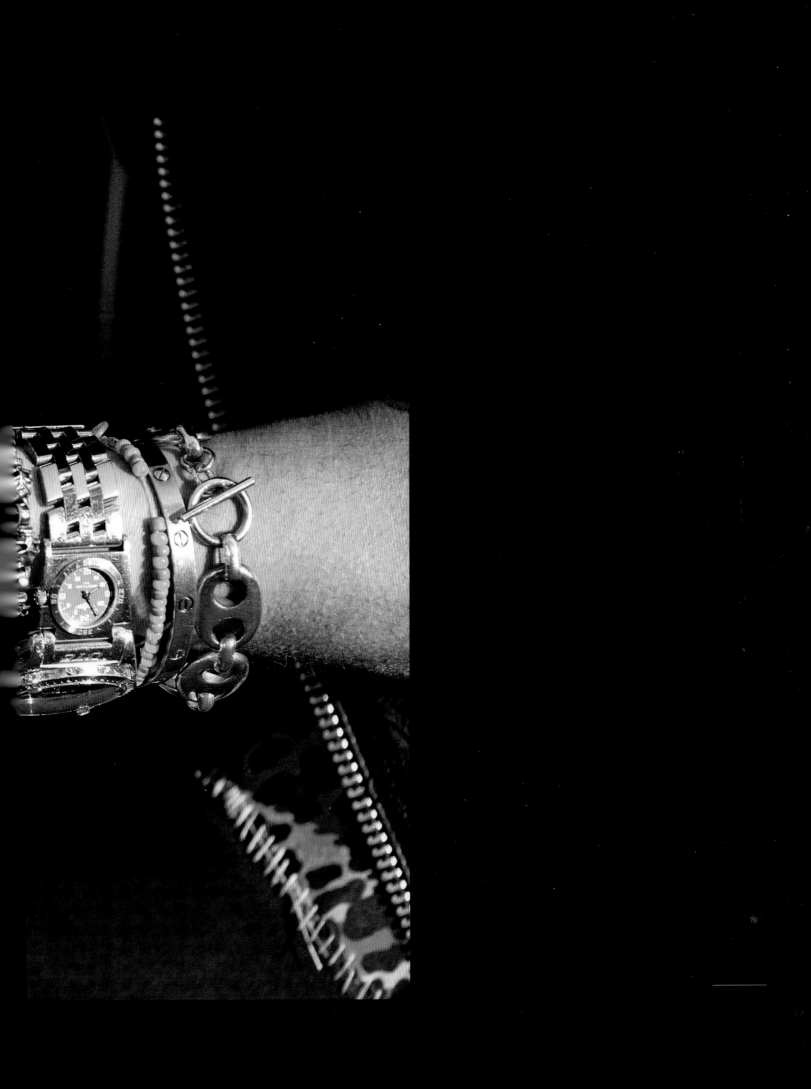

5

Portraiture

FROM A PHOTOGRAPHER'S STANDPOINT, Slash has everything you could ask for. The guy radiates rock and roll. And it's not fake. You can go out to a club in Hollywood any night of the week and see people in all their rock regalia—the jet-black-dyed hair, the tattoos, the boots, the leather—and you just think, Wow, that's really sad. Because it looks like a costume. But Slash just exudes this natural "It" factor. He lights up a room.

A static, solo shot is an ideal setup to give a true sense of what a striking figure Slash is. He's just eminently interesting from an aesthetic standpoint. He's also very easy to pose. He never resists. He's relaxed and lets you do what you want to do. He doesn't question it.

I haven't done much in the way of traditional studio shoots with Slash, with just him, me, and a plain white backdrop. This session from a few years back was one of those rare instances. The photos were to be used as wall art at various Guitar Center locations, and we took the shots in a studio adjacent to the Hollywood location on Sunset. Slash had just started promoting a new line of signature Les Pauls, and he posed with various Gibson and Epiphone versions of the guitar. He also picked up some of his older guitars, like his red Snakepit Les Paul. He was in all black, against stark white. Afterward, an artist friend of mine and I added some pretty strange graphics to some of the backgrounds. These wild images were then plastered on the sides of Guitar Center buildings across the United States.

Some of my favorite shots from this session are the silhouettes. You put all the light on the background and none on the foreground and you get nothing but a shadow. My thinking was, How many guitar players out there today can be presented in silhouette and people will know who it is instantly? I can't think of anybody else. You could put some pretty famous guitarists—or pretty famous *anybodies*, for that matter—in that scenario, and the truth is it might not be as easy to identify them as you would imagine. But with Slash the connection is immediate.

Occasionally I would get Slash alone for a more impromptu portrait shoot. In one instance, he was taking part in a Velvet Revolver press conference at the Chateau Marmont, and we stepped away and started shooting outside. It occurred to me that I had never done any tight facial profiles of him. So I zoomed in close and put the background out of focus.

I've always found Slash's face to be very revealing, which is maybe why you don't see it too often. To me, there's a profound sense of shyness about him. He can be pretty aggressive and outspoken, but when you home in on him, a gentler, more childlike person is revealed. What you see in those instances is what I imagine you would have seen when he was twelve years old, riding his BMX bike through the streets of LA.

When I had my studio at Third Encore, there was always something going on. Slash would be working in the building, or maybe nearby at another studio like Mates, and he would just pop in. These photos, from around 1999, are a good example of one of those quick sessions. Slash is standing in front of a backdrop that was painted by my wife. The shirtless shot was a pretty sexy pose for him. It's epic looking.

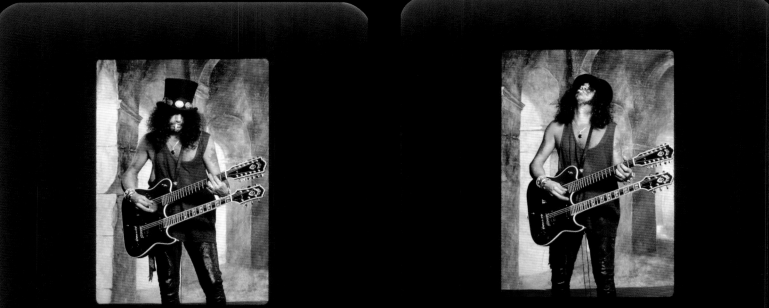

Around 2000, I was involved in helping to manage the Yardbirds, and I got them a deal with Steve Vai's label, Favored Nations. We put together their first record in more than thirty years and recorded it at the Mothership, Steve's studio in Hollywood. I thought it would be really cool to have the band redo some of their classic songs with different guitarists, and we got Steve, Joe Satriani, Brian May, and a few other guys to appear on the record. Slash played on "Over Under Sideways Down." He came in and laid down the most amazing guitar work. He was so excited to be playing on a Yardbirds album that he showed up thirty minutes early to the session.

This was likely another photo shoot done for Guitar Center, at Slash's former house in Beverly Hills. It was a great place, with a full recording studio, about a dozen Guns N' Roses pinball machines and a temperature- and humidity-controlled room for all his snakes. Eventually Billy Bob Thornton wound up living in that house. One day a few years later, I was there shooting Billy Bob, and I mentioned to him that Slash had previously owned the house. Billy Bob, said, "I know. One of his fucking snakes was left here and it got loose. We found it living up in the rafters!"

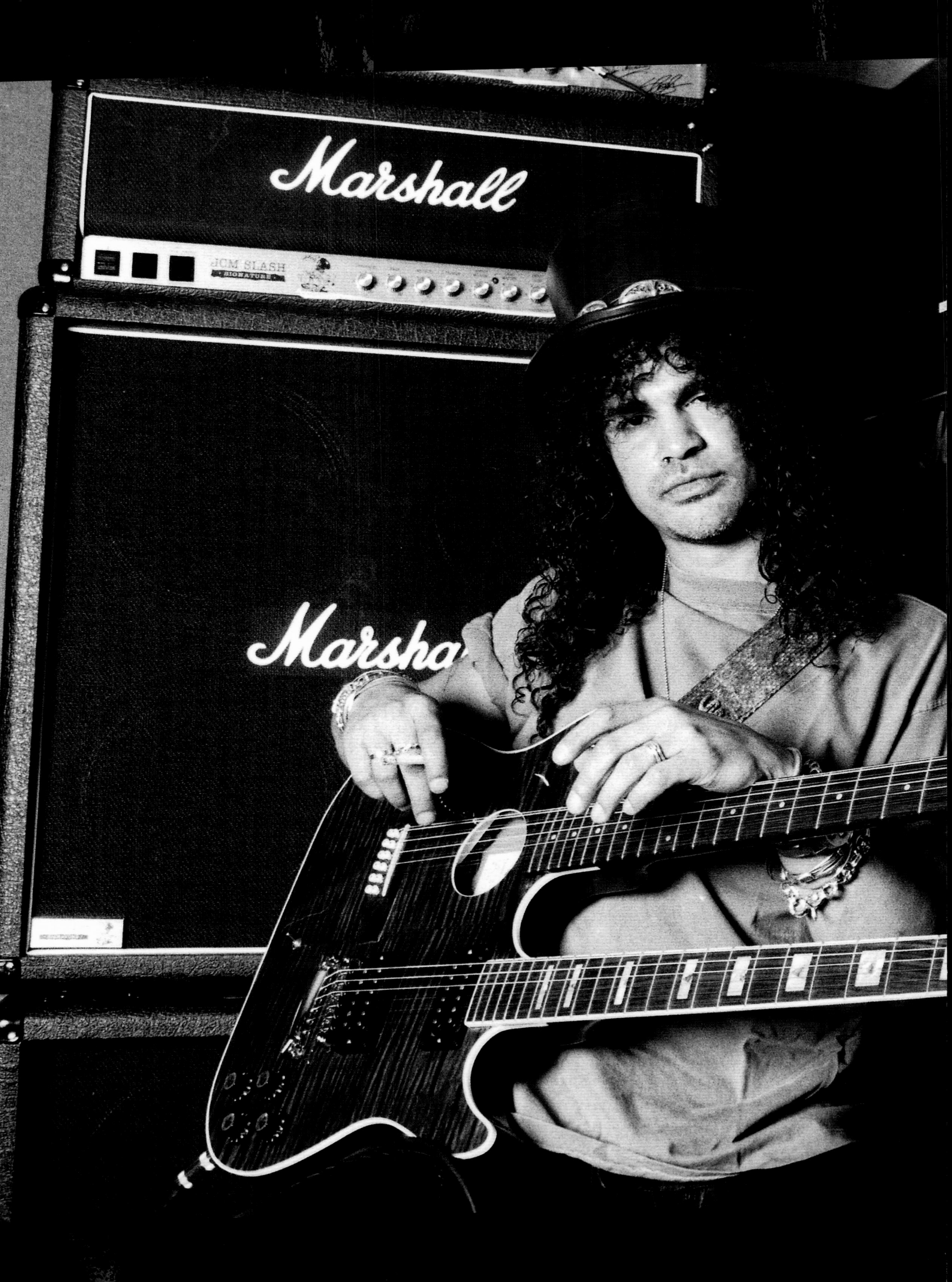
Marshall
JCM SLASH
SIGNATURE
Marsha

6
Recent History

IN A CERTAIN ARTISTIC WAY, I see Slash as very much like Jeff Beck. Beck has worked with some amazing people in his life, but he is driven to keep moving forward and evolving. Slash is the same way. His last solo album was an ambitious project, just for the sheer fact of bringing together so many different singers and personalities. Now he has a great solo band and seems to be really digging this thing he has with Myles Kennedy. I think he's found that musical camaraderie that had been missing in his life for some time.

In January 2011 Slash and his current band opened for Ozzy Osbourne at Mandalay Bay in Las Vegas. Watching him perform that night, it was obvious to me that something special was going on. In the past, there were times when he had seemed utterly frustrated onstage. But here he was alive. You could see this was real and very organic. The musicians fed off of one another's energy, and Slash and Myles had this great interaction. It was Mick and Keith. Steve and Joe. It's what Slash had been looking for.

Early in 2012, he took the band into Barefoot Recording in Hollywood to begin work on *Apocalyptic Love*. One day toward the end of the sessions, he asked me to come down to the studio. By this point the other members of the band were gone, and Slash was tracking guitar solos. It was a really relaxed vibe. He said, "Shoot whatever you want, and just let it happen."

We settled into the Slash Box, an enclosed area off to one side of the main recording room, where he cut many of his guitar tracks. It was a small space, not well-suited to having another guy standing there pointing a camera in your face while you played. But Slash was unfazed. He recorded live takes as I shot, which was pretty remarkable.

Later on, we took some photos by his gear. It was all very impromptu; I used the natural low light of the room and a high ISO. He stood in front of a rack of guitars, and it was all the classic stuff, like the Les Paul he used on *Appetite for Destruction*. I saw labels on cases from years back—Guns N' Roses, Snakepit, Velvet Revolver. It all stays with him. It's part of his lifeblood. He has these things around him at all times. It's similar to how he approaches the recording studio: he makes it look like his living room. You go into some of these professional studios and it's like you're in a museum, but with Slash, there's a certain chaos. A certain funk. It's more like a man-cave.

In February 2012 I shot Slash outdoors on the grounds of the mansion at MGM Grand in Las Vegas. He had just come off a weekend of really great shows, performing at a seventieth birthday party gala for Muhammad Ali and then the next night with Joe Perry at a Lenny Kravitz gig. He had guitars with him, but I didn't want them in the photos.

My idea was to present him as a normal person, for whatever that's worth. He was saying to me, "I don't know what to do with my hands!" The fact is, in many ways Slash is fully realized as a person when he has his guitar. There's not much he does that's not in the service of being a musician and an artist.

Which is why in some way, I suppose the greatest thing I can offer him as a photographer is to frame him within the same visual narrative as I have other iconic artists. In my eyes Slash is as relevant as a Jeff Beck, a Jimi Hendrix, or a Jimmy Page. He's as relevant as anyone. He's more relevant than most, in fact, because he just keeps going. I believe he has more enthusiasm today for what he does than he has had at any time over the course of our more than twenty-year friendship. He's still out there pushing, and I don't think he'll ever stop. I'm fortunate to be there with my camera to bear witness to it.

This show was the first time I saw Slash with his new band. I couldn't believe how great they sounded. And Myles blew me away. I knew that he had also been considered as the singer for the Led Zeppelin reunion that never happened, so to get the guy that Jimmy Page thought could stand in for Robert Plant wasn't such a bad thing for Slash. I shot their performance and then split. I didn't stick around for Ozzy. I had heard that on the second or third song of Ozzy's set, he hosed down the crowd with some sort of foam spray. So I took my camera and got out of the building.

Slash and I did this shoot in about ten minutes. He had a wedding to go to—his bodyguard, Junior, was marrying a good friend of Perla's. This is Slash's wedding outfit. He asked me to come with him and shoot the ceremony, but I had to say no. It was also my wife's birthday and she was waiting for me at a restaurant. I told him if I went to the wedding, I'd be getting a divorce!

photo by Maryanne Bilham

Acknowledgments

I would like to thank Slash and Perla Hudson, Richard Bienstock for his great words, Joe Perry, Ronnie Wood, Myles Kennedy, Jeff Varner, Raoul Goff and the whole crew at Insight Editions, Ray Scherr, Maryanne Bilham, Dave Weiderman, Gibson Guitars, all my guys at Nikon and MWW, and Dustin and the crew at Guitar Center Corp.

I want to dedicate this book to all the young guitar players around the world whose lives have been lifted by Slash and the legacy of his playing. To me Slash is the very definition of rock 'n' roll.

—Robert Knight

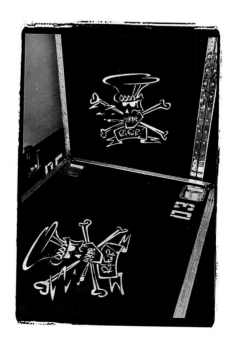

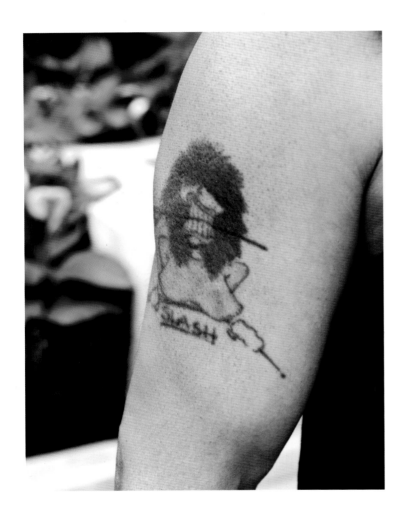

Colophon

Publisher: *Raoul Goff*
Acquiring Editor: *Robbie Schmidt*
Art Director: *Chrissy Kwasnik*
Designer: *Jon Glick*
Editor: *Chris Prince*
Associate Managing Editor: *Jan Hughes*
Production Manager: *Jane Chinn*

*Insight Editions would like to thank
Kris Branco and Jeff Campbell.*